Please return / renew by date shown
You can renew it at

Blue Movie

Blue Movie
Bobby Parker

ISBN: 978-0-9927589-7-4

Cover photograph © Matthew Wyndham

First published October 2014 by:

Nine Arches Press
PO Box 6269
Rugby
CV21 9NL

www.ninearchespress.com

Printed in Britain by:

imprintdigital.net
Seychelles Farm,
Upton Pyne,
Exeter
EX5 5HY
www.imprintdigital.net

Blue Movie

Bobby Parker

Nine
Arches
Press

new poets series

Bobby Parker was born in 1982 and lives in Kidderminster, England. Publications include the critically-acclaimed experimental books *Ghost Town Music* and *Comberton*, both published by The Knives Forks & Spoons Press. His poetry, artwork and photography have appeared in various magazines in print and online and he writes a poetry column for *The Quietus*. His reading style has been described as "Gripping, weird, relatable but alienating, emotional, totally fantastic poetry." by Café Writers. *Blue Movie* is his first full collection of poems.

CONTENTS

Isobelle... Emma...

Mom & Dad...

Factory Spirit

Tell your dad you are close to the beautiful poem,
living in a makeshift moon, running from evil
pictures. Don't compare prescription drugs
to a mother's hug or a daydream made of paper,
that will only make him angry. Let him think
you're stoned again, staring at your dirty feet
on the grass, wondering how to make him laugh
before it's too late for the tumbling sky
and his thin, white hair. He talks about the phantom
smell of wartime pipe-smoke on his night shift.
How he desperately longs to see the factory spirit,
to know there's something else before
they lay him off again. He'd like to see his mother.
He taps the table with a silver lighter, squints
at clouds that look like Christmas ghosts.
A robin on your neighbour's fence is holding
a small crucifix in its beak. Your dad sees it too,
but he doesn't say anything. You tell him sometimes
you wish you were a ghost, so that you could make him happy.
He sighs because the world is a headache; he doesn't know
what happened. He tells you that he drifts through the old
buildings every night, talking to the dark, until it's time
to go home. And for some reason it reminds you of love,
I mean it seems like your dad is talking about love.
And for a few seconds you can't remember
very much about your life, as you push your toes
under the cool soil and realise his lucky silver lighter
is broken, and that is why he isn't smoking.

The Opposite of Excitement

When I was young I frightened
my mother while she was hanging
white sheets on the line.
Ran at her with an evil face,
clawed hands like Bela Lugosi
growling *'Aaaaaaaaaaaaaarrrrrrrgh!'*
She jumped, but didn't scream
though almost burst into tears for fear
because I was such a wicked child.

There is a pain for me
thinking of the day I terrified her;
it runs along my arms and into my hands
making my fingers ache.
I think it comes from my stomach.
It is the opposite of flowers and
excitement, it is the opposite
of the day at the beach when she told me
how she met my dad and fell in love.

If I could take it back and replace it,
I would leave a son full of
birthday balloons and small candles
excellent school-reports and pictures
of stick parents on a piece of card
holding hands beneath a crayon sky.
I would tell him how short the time
is we get with mothers who smile.
And he would hang the sheets for her.

And the wind would blow through her hair.
And the wind would blow through her hair.

H.G. Wells

I pretended to be invisible, picking
up ashtrays and cups in slow motion
to frighten her mother – she gasped,
'This flat is too cold for me!' and as
her mother got up to leave I grabbed
her shoes, holding them just out of reach;
every time she tried to snatch them
was a minor victory. I did this until
she looked at my fiancée for justification;
then my fiancée looked at me, or the space
where I should be smirking, furious.

The vicar came round to talk about
the wedding. I ruffled his hair, twisted
his nipples and filled the room with phantom
laughter. Happy as a ghost I opened his bag,
found a soggy sandwich and slapped
his cheek with a piece of salami.
'Are you sure?' He asked. She took a deep
breath and nodded. He sighed.

I played this game until she couldn't stand it
any longer, 'I can see you! We can all see you!
Does this mean you don't love me?! Is this
your way of trying to get out of the wedding?'
So, with a click of my fingers I made myself visible.
We talked about mothers and vicars. We talked
about what's acceptable. Everything is okay now.
She has given me one week to replace
the smoothie-maker and kettle I used
to make my time machine.

No Screaming While the Bus is in Motion

It's true I pulled a wardrobe door
from the firewood pile and painted
a sign: *Parker's Ghost Hunting Agency*
in dripping red letters and nailed it
to the fence alongside our house
where passers-by pointed and laughed.
Kids threw stones at our windows.
A boy they called Bad Dog
blacked my left eye for lying.
My parents let the sign
stay up for a week
before my dad burned the fucking thing.
It was around this time I started
to think about death a lot, lying
in my imaginary coffin on the sofa,
arms crossed over my chest, holding my breath.
Quoting Freddy Krueger at the breakfast table.
Mum cried. Dad slapped me
and ripped Vincent Price
off my bedroom wall.
                    Such horrors;
before we moved up the hill
next-door to a girl
with green eyes.

The Other Boys

I told her about the other boys,
the sharp voice under my ribs,
how my head is stuck in lesser moments.
I told mum what touched me
as her mouth wobbled through hot tea;
a list of time-travelling drugs.
She sobbed, 'Why didn't you tell us?'
'Kids can't talk about sex,' I said.
'Especially not with their parents.'
She wouldn't look at me.
The waitress was called Dorothy.
I think it was a Friday afternoon,
late summer cooling after weeks of heat.
My baked potato was a clumsy fact.
The ceiling sagged all over us.

Particles

My wife assured me it was dog shit
on my trainers, crushed into the hallway
runners cut from mum's old carpet.
I thought it was human,
a smell that knew my name.
I washed my hands three times.
Our daughter rubbed the dark rings
around her eyes. 'Are you still my little
princess?' I asked. 'Yeah,' she said.
My throat is sore from shouting.
Maybe I'm sick like the others.
I left my trainers by the front door
then traced my steps looking for stains.
The stink made me think of insides.
The insides of a monster, perhaps, or
a man who doesn't want to go to hospital.
I sat on the bed pulling my thick hair.
Pulling and twisting it, cackling mad.
Then we cleaned the hallway
together, visualising shitty particles
vanishing like a tribal language.
Our flat was a place where love
sometimes cried for hours, hours
and hours and hours, while my shattered
wife sang *'Hush, Little Baby...'*
wearing her mother's tatty slippers
and a dressing gown that used to be white.

Sketch

His voice, a burning cigarette
lost in their bed sheets.

He turns her name into a Ferris wheel.

My dreams are full of sex.
In dreams I'll shag anyone,
people with skin like plastic bags
washed up on Blackpool beach.

Eyes that remind me to brush my teeth.
You get the picture.

But my friend, in the back of the car
whispering *Paris* to his girlfriend,
he's cool as a dealer's heart and will never know,

will never, never, be me
and that's what I was thinking while
everybody else discussed their favourite novel,

bright lights unravelling country lanes
and fog ahead of us all the way.

Signs of the Son

'Get on with it,' you say, as if it's a job.
Except there's no bread on the table,
only pills, fingernails and plastic cutlery.
My Valium stare burns beyond you, across
the red sea, searching for desert islands
with the same poisonous fruit as mine,
the same washed-up ghost ships.
You think this is temporary, stupid
sadness, a scab waiting to fall off,
as if it will shrink like a fat ass
if I give up junk, run when I feel mad,
star-jump through hell until I'm clean.
The furniture in my head is old
and broken. Some of it isn't mine.
I stop you swaying when we hug
because it's weird. Outside, the angry
street tortures itself with similar faults.
I struggle to answer your questions.
I point out the window and tap my skull
because they are the same.
'I understand,' you say, but you don't.
Sometimes you think I'm possessed,
studying my face for signs of the son
who, maybe once, smiled easily,
listened, loved your words like toys.
For a moment the sun strikes your glasses,
reminding me of medical lamps.
I let you kiss my cheek; pick up the truth
and carry it like a mouse: 'Get on with it…'

Heartbreak Delirium

My bedroom gathers
night traffic
footsteps through puddles
cars that never stop.

The first dream tells me
sex is a lake full of lost hooks
and headless toys.

The second dream disturbs me
her voice is punk rock
in a valley of pianos.

Listen to my heartbeat, it sounds
like someone throwing tins
of baked beans at an empty wardrobe.

A gate across the street
howls against the padlock.

Like peeling off Elastoplasts
is tonight's simile
for the sound of tyres in the rain.

Darker on the Floor

Nicky stared at me as I got down
on my knees to pick up my hair.
'It looks darker on the floor.' I said,
before spreading it across my palm
under the light of a cracked window.
She asked me what I was looking for.
I didn't know. My wife brought our
daughter into the kitchen; they smiled.
For a second I didn't know anything.
'Daddy looks much better now!'
Our daughter pointed over
my left shoulder, where nothing
was happening. Careful voices
asked, 'Does it feel better?'
'No,' I said. 'Just colder.' The urge
to stuff my dandruff-cursed hair into
a magic bag was nicotine-strong.
Fingers quivering like dowsing rods.
My family controls the weather.
It might have been the first day
of spring when my heart wandered
away from their worried blue eyes
until there was nowhere else to go.

Edwin

Laughing at his trainers in the changing rooms
look at my cheap trainers he chuckled
but the other boys
had big hairy dicks in the showers
one had a tattoo
on his fat red bicep
I thought it was a horse with an Afro
but it was a crappy wolf with the moon behind its head
Edwin shouldn't smoke weed because
paranoid
schizophrenia
because his older brother
smothered an old lady with a pillow
because of the cross he branded
onto his forehead
with a glowing butterfly knife
I remember his toothless parents
brought their collection
of snakes into school
stupid snakes laughed Edwin
look how poor we are
his parents had been wearing those same clothes
for weeks they smelled like forgotten groceries
but the other kids had sexy legs
and they said yuck
when our sassy biology teacher
squeezed green crap out of the dead pig's anus
and showed us X-rays

of her fat old thighs
I told my therapist that we used to stand
by the pond because Edwin felt peaceful there
I wonder why
I think about him so much.

Crossbow

His dreadful fingers filled the beer-can pipe
with crack. He passed it to me:
Slow pirate ship. Death-metal music.
My head tried to take off but there was
nowhere to go as my friend reached
under his bed and pulled out a crossbow,
tried to load it, stretching the wire back,
arrow in his teeth. Forgiveness; my flowers;
brain sweating and bumping into heaven.
I could see it clearly: the loaded crossbow
passing over my body until that dirty arrow
kissed my chest and the world turned red.
It was like trying to lift the sadness of factories.
The room squeezed my throat, played games.
A lonely girl was calling my name. Every now
and then I begged to see her. And every
now and then I begged her to go away.

3:06 a.m.

The sound of girls walking home
shouting from the clubs keeps my
left eye wedged between the blinds
they are so full of temporary happiness
and temporary abandon and temporary
ignorance that I want to run out there
and gather them into my arms like roses
but by the time I jump into my dying shoes
dig my smile out of the haunted wardrobe
and stumble through silent corridors
they will be gone and I will be just another
half-naked nutcase dancing for love
under the marmalade streetlamps.

Nightlife

When we crawl into bed
our furniture moves around.
Armchairs hover to switch places
with the table and sofa.
My desk drags itself into
the hall to brood in darkness
while the pine bookcase stares
longingly out of the window.

In bed we talk about things we
could never say in the light.
Our appliances come to life
and, as if pushed by unseen
hands, gather outside our
bedroom door to eavesdrop:
fridge-freezer and faulty cooker
moved by our sobs.

Come morning everything
is as we left it, but we know
what happens when we go to bed.
The world rearranges itself around us.
The sea swaps places with the sky,
trees waltz with gravestones.
Houses swim with the brightest stars

and someone luckier than me
and someone luckier than you
skates across the cracked ice.

Ducks Staring Into You

Ring him. Send him a text; just a couple of lines,
save the rest for Friday. It's almost pure!
How often do you get pure stuff? Lately it's been
half washing powder half something that isn't this.
It's only six minutes to midnight, you can be in bed
praying for sleep and biting your tongue with apologies
by 3 a.m. Kneel in the bathroom, chop it carefully
with your library card. Snort it off the toilet seat;
glance painfully at your daughter's bathwater
with blue ducks and yellow ducks staring into you
from bubbles that won't be there tomorrow.
A bath-time you missed, again. Another day's bathtub-echo
laughter gone, her two front teeth, golden hair.
Drink everything. Listen to heavy metal music.
Lean forward. Lean back. Sweat. Check your pulse.
Sit down. Walk into the kitchen, turn the light on.
Turn it off. Smoke a roll-up in ten seconds in ten-minute
intervals in the paranoid car park. Forget about
your wife's innocent leg hanging out the bed.
Your daughter, crawling faster with light to hug you
every morning. Every fucking morning. Smell her hair
and tell yourself, 'This is what makes me happy!'
You liar. You bastard father. You darkness.

Palpitations

1

This out-of-tune
relationship makes me deaf.
Snowflakes in my ears
the shadow of a monster
like a wild river between us.
It is the wrong kind of love
that keeps me calling.

2

Sunrise and traffic;
miniature balloons in
the dilated pupil.
It smiles and I can't breathe,
touches my chest and a million
shivers break the world.
Is this what you meant when
you told me to believe?

3

A kind of truth serum –
we drag secrets out of the cellar
examine their novelty hats
strip them under hot lamps
pass them around like pictures
of twentieth-century freaks –
do you really want to know why
my childhood was such a puddle?

4

I have a clear plastic bag
full of nostril scabs.
She has a life half-empty
like a new house waiting for
our stuff to silence the echoes.
If God will make you disappear,
you and your super bike
you and your black book,
I will cut the devil out of my poems
and fill these rooms with flowers.

5

The URGE: nothing else
only a promise like a pendulum
swinging through the sad brain.
Nothing else, only heartbeat
tingle-skin, that feeling you get when
you know she's going to come.
No, nothing, nothing, only
dreaming white against
the black screen of boredom.
She explodes in the makeshift
happy home and we jettison
everything but the lie.

6

Between the lines there's a life trying
to clear more space. It reminds me
of my grandfather raking leaves.
When I close my eyes to the sun it's
as if he's still here teaching me to count.
Showing me how to make a penny disappear.

7

Learning to slow down is
cold soup, night terrors,
a wife who wants to stay in
for the talent show.
It is a man sat on a hot stove
trying to picture all the beautiful
girls he went to school with.
It is throwing
imaginary stones
into a calm sea
forever.

8

Take this man
I mean this bad man
put him in a box
shove him under the bed
don't say his name.
Take this other man
I mean this good man
brush him off

prop him on the pillows
tell him he is wonderful.
As for the other thing
I mean the thing that made him bad
pretend it doesn't exist
like a ghost (ridiculous!)
like the end of the world (bollocks!)
now,
listen
listen
listen carefully
he is about to begin.

Best DAD in the WORLD

there was a man in the park today
he looked like the best dad in the world
his daughters' looping laughter on the swings
he smiled like it was easy
like it wasn't lifting a bag full of sad people
it was a red leaf blowing off the library steps
he was obviously
a very clean dad with lots of skills
such as fixing things
and making women happy
i considered flicking the shitty
baby-wipe off the bench
but the thought of it
made me feel angry at the mysteries of life
the man was goofing around he didn't
care who was looking
i studied his comic timing
memorised his clothes
not once did his handsome face
scrunch and flicker

with **a n**

x i e

t y

first the blonde daughter
kicked him up the arse
then the ginger daughter
kicked him up the arse
swinging and giggling
like it was crying
and falling.

Blue Movie

My friend's dad's bedroom had
a Betamax player with one tape inside.
One day, when the chocolate
was gone and nobody knew anything,
a few of us crept in and pressed play.
Funny music, pianos banging
madly under strings. A dirty old
man peeping through a basement window,
watching an overweight woman
gently masturbating. I think she was
Italian. She looked like somebody's mother.
Scattered around the bedroom
we yanked without shame or interest
in each other, only the naked woman
performing with reds and pinks
and wet teeth on a torn single mattress.
The old man was yanking too,
under rags that looked like dead leaves,
wheezing with popping yellow
eyes in the rain. Under the spell
of Blue Movie we wanked like athletes.
When the old man sneezed
she stopped, tilted her gorgon head
towards the window as the pervert
ducked then carried on until, peaceful,
she blew the candles out.
When the tape finished, boredom
was there like a dusty teacher

tapping his watch outside the school gate.
Later we wrestled each other
on the sunny front lawn
as my friend's pissed dad snarled,
'Little cunts!' flicking his stinking fags
under the ice-cream van parked nearby.

Jealous of Your Fighting Skills

To keep my heart from fluttering
panic blackout fear, I repeat the names
of high-school girls who laughed
through Art and Chemistry, the ones
with perfect legs in tights and lips
that cleaned the corridors. I hug
my medicine bag, careful of boys
with veins like poltergeist toilets
and cars that bollock round corners.
As I lean towards the hospital,
groping black coat pockets, I realise
I spend more time clutching keys
ready to stab scabby young twats
than I do smiling, or complimenting
people, or licking sugar off my lips.
With no alternative and another
hour walking these streets, counting
ugly beautiful terrible girls,
I poke the big one like the stub
of a worn out pencil through my soft
diazepam fingers and hold on until
what I'm afraid will happen, happens.

Dummy

My rundown wife interrupts this poem to ask
if we are watching the film tonight and I growl
Can't you see I am writing a fucking poem? Jesus!
and she says *SORRY* and I ask how I'm supposed
to write about my gambling addiction if she's going
to make me feel guilty about a stupid film
and she wails *I SAID I'M SORRY!* and runs
into the bedroom slamming the door
waking our baby daughter after we've just spent
an hour trying to get her to sleep and I sit here on fire
wondering if I should be the one to get up and do
the dummy thing or if my wife is going to get up
and do the dummy thing or if she will sulk for a while
waiting for me to apologise for being such a bastard
but then she drifts out of the cold bedroom
soothes our daughter back to sleep and creeps into
the living room to haunt me beside my writing desk
as I spit a lump of nicotine gum into the dust beneath
my desk lamp and begin with that crazy old bitch
on the next machine rubbing the screen begging
for sevens as a bright blue slot sucks our money away
and the arcade manager brings me crap coffee in a dirty
white mug and ten-pounds-worth of brass loyalty tokens.

Car Wash

1

I want my daughter's voice
without the background
hiss of hoses.
Her *I love yous*
like the earth-flash
reflection of passing birds
across a queue of dirty windscreens.

2

Wake up with the first
blast and wait for the engines.
Repeat the words *Car Wash*
using different accents
until my morning
boner wilts.

3

The man from Environmental Health
gave us monitoring equipment.
He said he lived
in a peaceful part of town.
When he talked down to me I stared
at his tie, 'Mate, that's a nice tie,' I said. 'Whew!
That's a fucking really nice fucking tie, man!'

4

Our daughter quietly
watches her parents
disassembling,
searching for glue.
I tell my wife I think we're coasting and we need
help.
Over her left shoulder
hooded figures count money
by the car wash gates, water
spraying through sunbeams,
hopeless sunbeams.

5

'Hey you! White boy prick! Why you
complain? You want us to come see you tonight?
Ha ha ha! We come see you and give you something...
Come over here, we talk about water. Look,
everybody love water. Everybody love a clean car!'

6

At night I stand outside, opposite
their locked gate, praying to evil magicians.
I talk to the dark wound above
these silent flats, turn my hands
into guns and shoot the blue rags they leave
to dry overnight
along the rusted spikes.
Snatch them!

Squeeze them in their sleep.
O Lucifer!
O Crowley!!
O Daily Mail!!!

7

She calls me dramatic.
I know she's right; it is only a car wash.
This prison cell can also be a bedroom.
This voice
something we can dance to.

8

Do they play cards in that caravan?
The caravan where they wait
on slow days.
Days of rain and peace.
I like to picture them playing cards.
Stopping when they think
they hear a car, footsteps, God's
whiny voice on the radio.

9

I tell my friend not to blow
kisses at the car-wash men.
She ignores me,
giggling.
I don't think they know
or care

that she used to be a man.
They stand very still and watch us
catching
snowflakes with our tongues.

10

I have seen too many
silent couples
smoking on the pavement
waiting for the boss
to give the sign their vehicle is clean
so they can go
wherever it is silent couples go
on Saturday afternoons
in stupid England.

11

I haven't been
stabbed yet
Mum.

12

Sorry Dad,
I write poetry.
I wrote a poem about a car wash.

13

The car wash is closed for the day.
I spoke to my doctor, she said I don't have to buy
medicine from smack-heads any more.
She put me on a prescription.
She said everything will be okay in the end.
And it's hard to finish
a poem about the car wash
across the street
when your doctor tells you
everything will be okay in the end.

The Thing

Steve shouted my name, tumbling through
crossroad traffic like Chaplin's Tramp. He was
still alive by the time he stopped in front of me
shivering outside the chip shop. He opened a plastic bag.
Three frozen joints of pork. Big joints
of pork like human heads covered in frost.
Tenner for this pork. Steve mimed injecting
into the pit of his right arm the way people mime
using phones or cradling babies, smiling, rolling his eyes
the way people do when they admit they drink a bottle
of red wine every night. The tenner in my pocket
held its breath – if I'm honest, you know, if I stand
in front of this with my trousers off, I wanted to ask Steve
to score me some gear, once he sold his pork
and made the call – the thing that lives behind
my heart like a homeless drunk with bad
tattoos of devils and dice on his rough yellow hands.
The thing that doesn't want me to wake up tomorrow.
A tenner in my pocket. When I got home I sat down on
the bed for a while until it went back to sleep. The thing.
I told my wife about Steve, the pork. I didn't tell her
about the thing. It frightens her because she doesn't
understand. You probably don't understand
but you can picture me with no trousers on.
My wife told my mum about Steve's pork and my
mum told her neighbours and everyone agreed
they would've bought the pork in a heartbeat;
my brain doesn't float like that, it moves
like a crab and thinks of ghosts of friends like Steve

pushing past me, in the direction of St Mary's Church
where we got married and christened our daughter
and wrapped red tinsel round the needle drop box.

Shut Your Mouth

Behind your smile there's
the kind of broken furniture
you don't want strangers to fix.

People want your secrets
to trade for more secrets until
the soul is a broken satellite dish.

Pretend your lips
have been glued shut
by a woman with red hair.

Keep the mischievous
flames of their tongues from
peeking into your petrol tank.

Communicate via nods and grunts.
If truth shines out of your eyes
wear dark sunglasses.

Cut out your mouth and throw
it off a bridge because it hates you,
it wants to pull you inside out.

When people ask your name
look away, shrug; consider it for
a moment – hold that thought.

Other Partners

I dance for you when
no one is around to
make me feel bad – people
who think dancing
is for music, good news
or exercise and not because
I know you like it
when my balls swing
against my jeans; I dance
because my body needs
to shake off the shadows,
shadows that have followed
me since I learned to lie, or at
least learned to hide the truth
by changing the subject.

Which reminds me, your
cooking is better these days,
a full stomach anchors me, keeps
me from straying beyond the lawn.

Isobelle 6 a.m.

No one has ever

been so happy

to see me

even though mornings

are strange and things keep

getting lost

I lift her out of the cot

she smells of

beautiful smiling piss

her strong little

fingers in my beard

every time she looks at me

a broken light-bulb

fixes itself.

Knots

Of course, my mother worries about me. She smells
of clean washing and blow-dried hair. She tells me
how much money comes in; how much money goes out.
She wants my dad to get a job. My flat is small.
When I stare out the window I want to break
the glass with my face. I take drugs and borrow money
for drugs – one time they thought I was going to die
but my friends walked me around in circles, opened
a window, stripped my clothes off and, dripping
like a treehouse in a rainstorm, I thought about my mother,
my mother, my mother. I thought about my mother
until I felt much better and took more drugs.
I'm suddenly aware how dark it is; how lonely
people sound when they laugh about drugs. So cold,
so scary now. It was not like this before.

The Silent Man

Our line drifted in the rolling humps
of green sea below the pier. Dad smoked
a stinking cigarette, indifferent, my moody
monosyllabic hero. The line tightened,
I slowly pulled a twitching crab
into our silent world and up
onto the pier, its pincers rattling on the cement.
We looked at it for a while. The sun
skipped off seawater puddles
and grinned inside my empty bucket.
We didn't know how to pull out the hook.
Dad cursed under his breath and nudged
the stupid crab with one of his holiday shoes.
He lifted it into the air. My mother
watched us from the beach, waving as she took
a photograph of father and son
holding a blurred problem between them.
He tossed the crab into the bucket
along with the line and the orange handle
and when he sighed, I sighed
and when the sky darkened, Dad's face
darkened, and when the rain touched my face
he lit another cigarette, started walking.

Snow Hill

I'm not sure this is going to be a poem,
Mum, but I've been thinking about anxiety,
how you passed it on to me and now
my daughter's face has that way of falling
out of the room when I'm madly rubbing
my chest, convinced it's the wrong shape.

I know you don't read poetry and I didn't
want you to think this is representative of
poems people write today. I want to clear
that up before we talk about the vision I had
on the train after they evacuated Snow Hill
station due to "a suspicious package".

It's not that this isn't a poem, I'm just
aware of being poetic and trying to avoid that,
typing fast with blurry eyes; I missed my test
maybe I need glasses, but people already say
how much I look like you, this anxiety
is enough and we burn easy in the summer.

This might be a poem depending on
who you ask. Dad thinks they should
rhyme but he bought you kitchen utensils
one Christmas and I remember feeling bad
for him, for you, banging new drums
in my cold shed at the bottom of the garden.

Don't think of it as a poem, forget
I mentioned poetry. I want to talk about
the vision I had on the train: I must have
forgotten who I was because when my mind
snapped back into the carriage I could hear
a heavenly choir loud as any concert.

No poetry – the other passengers didn't
seem to notice; I thought, 'How nice,
they are playing music through the speakers.'
but it got louder until the choir shook
the train and I could feel it climbing into me,
running through my veins like brandy.

I smiled Mum, and I'm smiling now, this
could be a poem! It was so pure I felt
existence communicating with me…
And then I realised it was just the sound
of wet tracks, metal slowing down, speeding
up, and the choir flew across the fields.

Maybe this is a poem but remember what
I said about poetry and don't show this to
Dad, remember the pots and pans. I'm sorry
for everything; you didn't know, but I know
and I can steer my daughter away from
this hand-me-down curse because I'm a poet.

It looks like this is a poem after all, Mum,
so you probably won't read it, or you will
pretend to read it and then talk about how
much you hate your life; that's okay, I won't
mention my vision if it will make you worry
about my future, the madness in my eyes.

So I wrote this poem for you, Mum, and for
myself listening to Chopin, grinding my teeth.
Slower and fatter and older now. My heart
is a dusty bell ringing in the hallway
of a house where no one speaks. My chest
is a funny shape. I hope I don't need glasses.

Flippers

If you are like me and you want to write
a poem but you can't because your heart
is a farmer kicking mud off his boots,
send me a photo of your mother's hands.

If you are like me and you want to paint
something you can sell but you can't because
your arms are cartoon arms, they change colour,
glue your empty purse to your right buttock.

If you are like me and you want to post
Meh... as a comment to everything your
Facebook friends think is cool or important,
cut off your hair, blow it out the window.

If you are like me and you want to sing
a blinder that makes your friends forget your
disgusting body, your disgusting face,
leave her laughing in the cold cinema.

If you are like me and you want to write
a poem but you can't write a poem
so you begin a poem with the words
"If you are like me and you want to write"

If you pull the skin back and tell yourself:
This hole is not full of old messages.
This hole is not full of other poets.
This hole is not the pain of leaving home –

If you are like me and you have to write
poetry because you're too scared to sleep,
too scared to stay awake watching telly,
too scared to tell her the truth about sex,

we should flip a coin to decide which one
of us is going to stop breathing first.

Fuck the Moon

Every other poem has the fucking moon
blaring from the centre, makes me sick!
My coughing blood wakes the neighbourhood.
My wife leaves the room when I see the moon
because she knows we're about to lose
some more furniture. Leave the moon alone.
Give us your head; peeled, colourful, half-asleep.
We have been eating the moon since high school.
Our bodies are weak, they need meat,
gristle and hot fat. They can barely stand.
We have overdosed on the moon; caught exotic
diseases, genital warts, spent nights in jail
with your fucking moons up our arses.
Give us strange spices, a flash of bone
from your skeleton lockers. Leave it alone!
The next time you find yourself writing
about the moon, stop. Go for a walk in the dark.
Call your mother and tell her you are sorry.

Poem in Which You Blame the Demon

Your friend thinks you are possessed by a demon
he says he told his church about you
and they agree
but they won't cast the demon out
because you are not a Christian
if they exorcise the demon
you would become an empty vessel
the demon will come back with his friends
their uppers are your downers
they will have a party inside you
their joy is your pain
your friend swears he saw
your eyes turn completely black
black as amateur porn
loading on a laptop full of viruses
he says Jesus Christ will take your anxiety away
if you stand in front of all these people
and upload your memory to God
the demon will piss off
and Jesus will do the washing up
but you don't step forward
you
shake sweat pop pills stare at the shape
of your shadow on the world
everyone is dancing
they remind you of scarecrows
bobbing in a hurricane   after the event is over
people wearing yellow t-shirts
bring food from a local takeaway

you watch the fat pastor
dangle a steaming slice of kebab meat
over his happy mouth
the meat makes a slimy sound
as it slaps around the pastor's lips
you stare at his pretty wife
think about her kicking you in the balls
imagine she's suffocating you
with her quiet Christian vagina
maybe the demon puts these thoughts in your head *yes*
just blame everything on the demon
the inside of the circus tent the church has rented
is dripping with condensation
and after walking in a circle with your head back
mouth open like a baby bird
you finally catch a drop of condensation
on the tip of your dry tongue
it tastes like some kind of fetish
your friend says only eight people stepped forward
and gave their hearts to God tonight
they were led away to the special area
where counsellors give advice
and start-up packs
and carefully folded emotions
they touch your arms and smile
for a moment you thought you might step forward
and wave at everyone
and cry a little bit
and walk to the special area
as the demon screams
No No No please No No
you almost ran towards the stage to hug the preacher

wailing your sins like the comedown crows of Sunday morning
perched on your neighbour's chimney burnt letters barking
the charred syllables of love Yes
a small part of you
maybe one of your nipples or a broken tooth
or the fading memory of your ex-girlfriend the lap dancer
regrets not stepping forward
because you feel guilty about a lot of things
such as mood swings and selfishness
seagulls and supermarkets
the way your mind wanders off
and yesterday you ripped up your wife's anniversary card
during an argument
and spat on each crumpled Hallmark half
you horrible bastard
your self-hatred is a gambler's guide to astrology
a fairground by the river
your childhood heaven's faulty jukebox
you wonder how the demon feels
when you take your daughter to the park
and you spin together on the big spinny thing she loves
and she looks around in awe
and then she looks up at you in awe
and tells you *this is fun I am*
having a great time with you daddy
as you push the spinny thing faster
and the park gate blurs into trees
and trees melt into sky
and sky shivers into sun
and the sun sets
behind the circus tent
and the pastor is happy

and his wife's vagina is happy
and your friend is studying
your demon eyes very carefully
as you log in to Facebook
on your crappy phone
because your lift is late
and you're not sure about this
you don't know if you are awake today
but you are definitely alone
you don't know if you are possessed by a demon
but you are definitely going home.

Jellyfish

There's no doubt she thinks he's lost at sea.
A smudge of blood on her glasses.
She looks healthy. She wishes he looked healthy.
Her weird stare drifts across his sick face
the shadow of a murder weapon
they called love.
Her new boyfriend is a taxi driver.
He is a quiet man with at least
one tooth missing, so obviously he's a paedophile.
When their little girl says the new boyfriend's name
her father's fingertips go numb; he has visions
of the taxi driver's dismembered corpse
scattered on a grey beach full of baby jellyfish,
broken phones, the nights he dies without her.
They share a joint in his parents' garden,
negotiating a future that bites too hard.
Her saliva moist on the roach, he takes the spliff,
inhales, wonders if this is the last time her spit
will touch his lips. The word *divorce* is sharp:
sound of sirens, fire alarms, flying saucers shining
through a nightmare of winter trees.
He stares at her chest, the cleavage
that may as well be a crack in his bedroom wall,
thinking maybe the sun will explode
if he reaches out to touch her; that she might hold
his haunted hand tight against her heart until it gets dark,
and tell him their marriage was a message
that failed to send, and tell him their daughter

is a dream, and tell him to go dig a hole
far away from here, as their tears scatter like silver
shrapnel through his mother's evil flowers
and all the sorry gardens beyond.

Heroin Lullaby
(or *Open Letter To My Wife Upon Our Separation*)

Now that we are separate ghosts, I hope at least
one of us can make the living scream,
learn how to shapeshift, throw a poltergeist
wind into the bleeding world. I noticed the mirror
I hate is back in the hallway, and you've stopped
asking me to do stuff. You look after our daughter,
look after me, cook, clean, change cat litter,
feed Keith the Goldfish that hates me...
You do everything – *without you things would
actually die.* All I do is sleep, melt potent downers
under my sore tongue, occasionally wanking
half-heartedly onto my least favourite t-shirt.
You pay bills, visit my folks and fetch the shopping.
I daydream about heroin the way some people describe
their mother's cooking, or how it feels to cum so hard
you temporarily go blind and lie laughing beside a girl
with eyes like eerie twilight coastlines.
Marriage – parenthood – I knocked once
for YES when maybe I should've flew back
into the skull we used as an ashtray. You kissed
the wine-stained Ouija board; I slapped a silver crucifix
off the wall. You shook the house until our daughter's toys
fell into the hole we dance around, the big fucking hole
of us, getting bigger every day, currently the size
of two sleeping lovers curled into a perfect spoon.
Yes, now that we are separate spirits, howling
and rolling desperate nights between our ringless
fingers like squidgy black dope, I hope one of us

can appear smiling in a photograph.
Prove that something else exists.
Maybe even save this... Of course, I feel
guilty about not doing anything around the house,
I'm due to leave any day now, but since you stopped
asking I've become so lazy and self-absorbed.
I think crap like 'what does the word SORRY
remind me of?' (a perfectly round, razor-thin
sheet of glass, spinning above the bed).
I stand at the top of the stairs in my filthy blue
dressing gown and lean forward a bit,
then a bit more, flirting with the fall,
listening to you make our daughter laugh,
singing lullabies and praising her sharp little mind.
This tapping on my teeth with the point
of a sacrificial knife! It hurts so much
my thoughts are like the horrid steam I saw
rising from a bald man's head in karate class
when I was ten years old and terrified of aliens.
It hurts so much I think my skin is dangerous.
The pain of leaving when you don't know
for sure. I worry the angels want to rub me out
and replace me with a brilliant pencil sketch of hands,
just two loving hands, holding each other, you know
the way, like under a table with candles perhaps,
or between those awkward airport chairs,
or in outer space watching the earth change colour,
burn off, and fade like a vicious love-bite, reminiscing
about good times until we run out of oxygen
and silently drift apart in the shimmering ink
of infinite mystery, our phones full of text messages
we couldn't bring ourselves to delete, the summer

photos and giggling videos. Those heart-stabbing notes to self: 'Help them more', 'Buy her flowers', 'Never be the one who turns out the light'.

ACKNOWLEDGEMENTS

Acknowledgements are owed to the following publications, in which some of these poems first appeared:

Astronaut Zine, B O D Y Literature, Dead Ink, Fit to Work: Poets Against Atos, Ink Sweat & Tears, Lung Jazz anthology (Cinnamon Press), *Magma, Orbis, Poems In Which, The Quietus, Stride, Under the Radar.*

'Palpitations' was published as part of on-line chapbook *Holograms of Rotten Roses* (Silkworms Ink)

Special thanks also to Angela France, Melissa Lee-Houghton, Daniel Sluman, Richard Scott, and the rest of my poetry family – without whom there wouldn't be a *Blue Movie*. Thanks also to my Kidderminster family: Tom, Matt, Dale, Sarah, Sean, Slippers, Katy, Cozza, & The Boars Head.